SISTER PROMETHEUS

Discovering Marie Curie

*For Sara —
I hope you find something
here that is a discovery.*

Sister Prometheus
Discovering Marie Curie

Douglas Burnet Smith

Winnipeg '08

WOLSAK & WYNN

© Douglas Burnet Smith, 2008

No part of this publication may be reproduced, stored in a retrieval system or transmitted, in any form or by any means, without the prior written consent of the publisher or a licence from The Canadian Copyright Licensing Agency (Access Copyright). For an Access Copyright licence, visit www.accesscopyright.ca or call toll free to 1-800-893-5777.

Cover art and design: Rachel Rosen

Typeset in Garamond

Printed in Canada by The Coach House Printing Company

Wolsak and Wynn Publishers Ltd
69 Hughson Street North, Suite 102
Hamilton, Ontario L8R 1G5

The publishers gratefully acknowledge the
support of the Canada Council for the Arts,
the Ontario Arts Council, and the Book Publishing Industry Development Program (BPIDIP) for their
financial assistance.

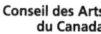 

Library and Archives Canada Cataloguing in Publication

Smith, Douglas, 1949-
    Sister Prometheus : Discovering Marie Curie / Douglas Burnet Smith.

Poems.
ISBN 978-1-894987-28-8

For Théo

CONTENTS

Poland 1860-1891   11

Paris 1891-1906   27

Half-Life 1906-1914   55

Les Voitures Radiologiques:
The Great War 1914-1918   73

Sister Prometheus 1918-1937   83

Le Panthéon, I: Installation, 21 April 1995

"To the Fatherland's Great Men, in Gratitude"

Above us, Foucault's proof: the earth moves precisely around itself 11° per hour, marked by the arc of his pendulum that sweeps slowly its silver-tipped ball through the box of sand on the black-and-gray-diamond floor above these crypts, as if trying to hypnotize *Les Grands Hommes de France* with 50 metres of steel cable – proof, also, that the dead still move, though quite dead, their indivisible atoms convulsing in perpetual revolution. Pierre & I converse side by side with Voltaire & Malraux, Jaurès & Gambetta. The rest of them ignore me, & shun Pierre because of me. (Remember, I'm the only woman down here.) They're fond of quoting themselves, especially on the subject of female intelligence, how it contaminates their world: "First it was the respectability of the Sorbonne, the good name of Science. And now, on all occasions, France." And so, Pierre & I dance, & share the last, eternal laugh, since it turns out that my demure but irrefutable presence here, & not the clever equations of Foucault, makes the great men rotate in their marble graves.

Poland 1860-1891

Wedding Photo:
Wladyslaw Sklodowski, Bronislawa Boguska, 1860

How noble they both look. They have tried to mask national humiliation with carefully constructed smiles. In one corner of my father's smile, there's the village he'll be banished to because he won't practice the Czar's customs, just to advance himself. The village is wrecked, empty, nameless. Under my mother's eyes are dark craters a bomb has left in Badusky Street. The eyes themselves are the same gray-blue enamel of the Vistula, & the hours that entirely compose my first memories of the world are the hours when her eyes would follow rhymes on a page until the rhymes turned into dreams of my father's hand shaping impeccable numbers on a slate. They stand there in the photo, before any of us was born, dissolving, & trying not to dissolve by smiling, by holding hands, by believing the sulphur flash & smothered explosion under the photographer's cape will preserve only them, all of their love & none of their shame, & nothing of the soldiers they hear marching in the square outside, orders barked out in Russian, & echoing in Russian, as they join hands & mean to smile.

Warsaw, 7 November 1867

    Russian sentries keep a sleepy watch over the red-brick hulk: Alexander Citadel. It looms high in wavering torchlight above the Vistula twisting frigid through the old-town below. The Czar's agents crush out cigarettes in some smoky café in Saxon Square, listening in Cyrillic for midnight plots. Listening for more Polish revolt. There are only the bells of seven churches perfecting the square, & wind lifting the first drifts of winter toward the knees of Copernicus, who broods there over a hollow world he holds in both bronze hands, tilted as far away as a world can tilt, in the refitted laboratory of his snowy universe, cold & remorseless as the season. Encamped at the gate of Royal Castle, white tents breed & billow around the misery of Russian troops trying to find warmth in banked fires, fingers stiff as triggers. They can see the glow of oil-lamps behind the wrought-iron balconies of Hotel Europyski, where the Viceroy is dining with the angels adorning Bellotto's rococo ceilings. They know the angels' pink, puffed-cheek blasts must be warming cognac in cut-glass decanters. They're waiting for the order to shoot at first light dead silent "The First Five," for reciting patriotic poems at the head of the unarmed crowd on Nowy Swiat, New World Street. The command comes from the bed of the Viceroy's mistress. Unsatisfied, she condemns the five dead to hang along the length of the sword of King Zygmunt, drawn hapless 200 years in Market Square. The rest are whipped stumbling in chains to Siberia & the luckiest are the hundreds who will become meals of thawed flesh next spring for the hundreds who will follow, & unfortunately live. In the midst of this official "Russification," under the sign of the horseshoe, the arrow, the cross, on Freta Street, the fifth of five, I was born & named immodestly after the Black Virgin of Czestochowa: MARIA SALOMEA SKLODOWSKA.

Typhus, 1874

I looked at the dispossessed face of my sister, hands folded in absurd serenity, her long, urgent bell-shaped body indifferent now, even to her best dress, a green husk of the newest piece in Heaven's jigsaw.... It's impossible to die when you are fourteen! I wanted her to smile. "Zosnia, tell us one of your stories," I wanted to say, but the parlour's silence was too pure, & my father's face, which that day looked as though it were made of cheap glass, could not have withstood the slightest sound, so I let my wish glide out the door into the street, to be run over by a tram, whose bell was there & not there for my father, as his daughter was there & not there; whose bell was a visitation from the Angel that arrives like a memory of winter & swirls through a house, a city, a country, gathering the required number of souls to complete the puzzle, my Uncle's withered voice said, as we rode in a coach through the cemetery, & with each soul, with every piece of the puzzle, a star comes on in Heaven, a sign the soul has arrived, a sign God's puzzle is more complete, he insisted, against his own loss of breath, against the dust we were raising, which was falling around us on the numberless headstones that showed, even to a child, that the arrival of the Angel had been completely unnecessary, stupidly pointless, & that the Angel must by now be bored, & very tired.

Tuberculosis, 1876

    Every morning I would see the previous night's pattern of blood on my mother's pillow, sometimes dark, like a rose, sometimes lighter, like the colour of the rash that had covered Zosnia's arms & neck & face. It gave off a smell like the smell of old grass at the base of a tree. Nothing was ever said about the blood. The blood was merely resented, as if it were a poor opinion no one had asked to hear: that a mother was no more important than the stain on a linen pillow-case; & doctors' opinions were just leaves falling into the long grass at the base of the tree, giving it that sweet, disagreeable odour. I would look up from the book I was reading & see the pillow-case, stainless on the line, lifted a little by the wind as it dried, my mother under the Dutch quilt asleep in a chair in the unconditional sunlight, exhausted from another night of coughing. She would always wake the moment I looked up from my book, & then, with the wearied beauty of habit, quietly tell me to go back to my studies, that the task I had before me was sacred: to make Poland proud of my achievements. But then there would be the moment just after, the moment when I'd look up knowing she'd be asleep again, knowing the pillow-case would be perfectly still in a lapse of wind, my mother's head fallen to one side, her mouth hinged slightly open, not even the scraping of a branch making the smallest protest against the right of my mother to sleep, of me not to read, & of the pillow-case, still & stiff, to be clean of even the faintest fleck of blood.

BIRTHDAYS

Mother abstained from the cherry wine on my sixth birthday & sipped *koumiss*, fermented mare's milk, the sour Tatra "cure." But her coughing could not stop, not that day, nor after long months absent, drinking ice-water in the Austrian Alps. She passed winters in the useless sun – Nice, Monaco, back to Nice. A final year of gasping, exile in the quaint air of Salzbrunn, one last summer in the needle-forest of Gdynska before her return to the damp dust of Warsaw. I turned ten the day she summoned us to her bedside. We kneeled, & she made a sign of the cross above our heads. She could not speak. She dropped her hand. The next night she was dead.

OBSERVATIONS, I

And so they both had vanished, sister & mother. Vanished from inside the clothing of their names, as if they had deserved to vanish; as if they had been expecting to vanish all along & had been in touch with whatever was making them vanish & loved it more than they loved those who said their names to try to stop them from vanishing, & kept on saying the names even after they were gone. So that the irretrievable became their names – *Mama, Zosnia*.... When Papa pronounced them, in remembrance, they were pronounced with a solemn grimace, as if the names were the prayer itself, a singular chorus intended to retrieve *wife, mother, daughter* from the realm of their abstraction, to return them to their bodies, if only to give them back the feebleness of their hands.

"THE SCALE OF DIGNITIES"

By proclamation of the Czar we said our morning prayers in Russian, profaning what we reverenced. And when the Inspector arrived, always unannounced, bursting into the classroom, Mademoiselle Sikorska would calm us with her eyes. This day, the Inspector pointed at me, spat his commands:

"Name the Czars who have reigned over our Holy Russia since Catherine II!"

Catherine II, Paul I, Alexander I, Nicholas I, Alexander II.

"Tell me the names & titles of the members of the Imperial Family!"

Her Majesty the Empress, His Imperial Highness the Cesarevitsch Alexander, His Imperial Highness the Grand Duke…

"Enough! What is the title of the Czar in the scale of dignities?"

Vielichestro.

"And my title – what is it?!"

Vysokorodye.

"And who rules over us?"

His Majesty Alexander II, Czar of all the Russias.

He spun out the door, on to another classroom. Mademoiselle Sikorska's face was white.

"Very good Maria. You may sit down." She turned & wrote the date on the blackboard. A wave passed over everyone's head.

On the way to school, Gymnasium No. 3, 1879

Even though I was a wise girl almost flowered out of the membrane of childhood, Kazia made me hold her hand along Krakowskie Przedmiescie because water-barrel wagons rumbled too close to the trolley kiosks & the coachmen of closed carriages liked to whistle & flick gaslamps with their whips. On the cobblestones of the square in front of Saxon Palace, Kazia showed me how to spit on the Czar's obelisk without being seen by the two-headed eagle on its gold-leaf perch at the top. In spring, we'd cut through the gardens & carry the scent of lilacs with us beyond the iron gates, a cloudy weight that would slow us down just enough so that we'd have to stop, check the time in Wosinksi's window where the watches from Geneva were set an hour behind. We'd dawdle, pretending we had all those minutes to walk to the convent doors, say the prayer, then swear our allegiance to the Czar, salute his precious flag. One morning that flag was draped half-mast, & after the prayer the convent bells rang & did not stop. A bomb in St. Petersburg had delivered Czar Alexander II to his examination by the angels. Knowing he'd fail, Kazia & I danced gleeful in an empty classroom. Mademoiselle yanked us by the braids to the office of the Superintendent. But he already knew I'd win the gold medal, & merely sent us home with stern letters of instruction on how to properly mourn the nation's loss. So we did, in secret, with lemonade & chocolate ices.

Lesson

    I was thirteen, & Witold Romochi put his hand on mine in the glass veranda at Micki. We climbed up to the tower room & the resinous heat underneath us, of drying peas, also climbed, & stroked our backs. Thunder was moaning in the Carpathian foothills. Wild gusts sent us back down, frightened by violence into silence. On the tidy path outside – a dead cuckoo. Dead from having seen through something it couldn't really see. Dead from having thought that hard glass was air.

SECRET SNOW, SECRET DANCE:
THE CARPATHIANS, WINTER 1884

    At sixteen, I danced an exquisite *oberek* at Skalbmierz, my legs kicking high my petticoats, torso rigid as a top-handle under the white blouse & beaded vest belling out over the embroidered waist. I was Maiden of Honour & led the *kulig*, in the first sleigh, my partner a handsome boy from Cracow. We danced from house to house, past dawn, ending with the white mazurka, the sleigh-driver so happily drunk we skidded off the torch-lit path, bells clanking, into the deep drifts, peacock feathers in the boys' hats sailing out over the snow.

Evening, after school, 1886

    A single Polish phrase, whispered in a hallway between classes – by student or teacher – & overheard by the Director, this could be your death-sentence, & your family's death-sentence. So, crossing our apartment's threshold every evening was crossing a border from the country of No to the country of Yes. One evening I was broken with fatigue (it had been the final day of the final year's oral examinations, in Russian) & I forgot which language belonged where. During dinner, in some sentence going astray, I said "in the first time." Papa put his fork down. I waited for the spring in his tongue to uncoil. I searched the table-cloth for camouflage. "Maria, 'in the first time' is a Russianism which violates the purity of our language. To finely-tuned ears it sounds like the groan of a sick cat. Please, do not make this mistake again. In Polish, it is '*for* the first time.' We must keep our language polished, like a gem." Words were the nation's diamonds. They sparkled and cut, compressed in the darkness of Polish history. We mouthed them in secret, like spies, waiting for the moment when a syllable would no longer be treacherous, a tongue no longer lethal.

THE CHAPEL OF THE VISITATION, 1887

    I came in out of the paperweight snow & saw Hela Wulf, her blue eyes streaming, & Anya Rottert's flat nose running, her chest heaving with sobs. We were on a retreat & I supposed Sister Helena had once more decided *someone has offended our Lord someone must be punished.* But then I saw Léonie Kunicka, crumpled, slumped against the door under the arch of the nave. Anya whispered, "It's Léonie's brother. He was found out in a plot. They are to hang him tomorrow." We 'kept watch' all night with Léonie. At dawn we fell on our knees & prayed. Léonie said there was no use praying, & cursed because she knew there was no one listening, especially the newly dead.

The Cascade, Mount Rysy, 1888

   Hiking in the Tatra Mountains, pale skin of the moon rising in the south, Maciej Skiewicz wanted me to play Sweet Desdemona to his Otello, & lie down like a bleating lamb & be grateful for being smothered with his affection into a comfortable dullness, silenced into nullity. Even then I had thought there was a small chance I could love him until, at the cold cascade, where the muscles of my calves winced in the current, he pronounced all women's education unnecessary, his strenuous intellect marching his reasons in an impressive column ahead of us, along the trail. When he'd finished with a flourish the last of his metrical rhetoric, he put a gentle hand to my cheek, & pledged a life's protection. I thanked him, rising to resume the ascent, & splashed a palmful of the pure, perishable water on my face, twice, where his hand had touched it.

Floating Academy, 1889

"We have learned how to die intelligently, but never how to live intelligently."
  – Aleksander Swietochowski

I read Goncharov & Dostoevsky, translated Heine, & La Fontaine, & Coppée, adored Orzeszkowa, though little good it held against the Positivists who loved to quote Comte's belief in the "natural inferiority" of women. So I took my books to the mountains & became a petty governess for three years in one bourgeois house of spoiled children after another. I became a chapter in *Miss Antonina,* the woman who careens from one landowner to the next, trying to forget, with the lamp burning all night in some sparse room, the discoloured photograph of a young man's face suffocating under her pillow; trying not to say to myself, like her, "You see, everyone has some little poem in her past…" though for me the poem was *learning*. And then I received a letter & books from Bronia – Daniel's *Physics* Spenser's *Sociology* (in French) Paul Bers' *Lessons on Anatomy and Physiology* (in Russian) – manna from Paris.

Paris 1891-1906

Sainte la ville où brule ce feu de laboratoire!
Claire Malroux

Vienna-Warsaw Station, November 1891

For the first few hours there was light enough to peer through the grimy pane as the hairline of Warsaw receded into the past. I must have been turning twenty-four as the train evaded the last lop-sided houses, spewing dangerous sparks onto thatched roofs. In the distance, dimly-lit towns, ruined castles, churches, always churches, & never ruined. I covered my legs with my mother's quilt. I ate the little bag of caramels Papa had given me, & dozed in the sugary dark. At Skierniewicz the tracks veered northwest & sliced through what by now, in the rising day, I could barely see – trees like oars terraced above the Vistula – then it veered again, more northerly, at the Russian-Prussian border. All of us seemed to wake at once, on our tiny stools in the 4th class Ladies Carriage, as we shunted through a maze of rails into Berlin. Later, far off, we could see two spidery towers, & knew we were passing Cologne & would soon nose along the French border. It wasn't until the morning of the third day, gray & vast as a sea, that we hissed & spumed under the thick glass of the Gare du Nord. And it wasn't until after the passing of a long, numbing week, having taken lodging with slaughterers from the stockyards near la Villette, in Little Poland, that I hoisted my skirts up spiral iron steps & like a dizzy queen watched Paris go by from the Impériale, the upper deck of the omnibus. I signed forms at the Sorbonne, shakily, but ever more firmly, "Madamoiselle," then walked down the hill of rue St. Jacques to the Seine, & Notre Dame. I was here, *un peu dépaysée*, but here, vaguely praying, hungry pigeons gurgling at my feet.

OBSERVATIONS, II: rue Flatters, 1891-1894

    Five landings, six storeys, exactly one hundred and one wooden stairs – grasping the handrail in the dark, I'd reach my little room under the cold, slanting, zinc roof, fumble for the alcohol lamp that allowed only a dimly strict aura of my second beginning in Paris fifteen minutes (instead of an hour) from the Sorbonne, & devotion to detail in the classroom, the laboratory, the library – detail the Absolute everyone rose to. All things aspired to equation: one egg equalled four hours' sleep; evening rain equalled dank sheets. From my miniature window, I could see the dome of Richelieu's chapel, & I'd think a century back to its sacking, his bones smashed (for some lost revolutionary cause) against the walls of his tomb re-named "The Temple of Reason." It squats now in the shadow of the Observatory where they confirm the age of the rare stars I watched shivering in the winter sky. The eye determines the stars, yes, but I wondered, what determines the eye? I loved to wake to the murmur of pigeons, their necks rainbowing the darkened dawn, their necks' vibrating embers the only warmth in the continual drizzle. Wings grey as December & January, months where the day-sky over Paris was a stalled sea, its tide-shine scoured dull in the clouds, not even a scrap of the moon to tint its silt silver. My sound fascination with them had something to say about magneticism – to be separate, apart but always drawn to something & away from something else – promise & extinction of promise, a structure that does not impose but *permits* its own dispersion – the dispassionate piecework of angels (gray wings against gray sky) flying all the way back to the black beginning.

"I TAKE THE SUN AND THROW IT …"

So le professeur, Monsieur Appell, concluded his lecture on Mathematics with his slight Alsatian accent, *pince-nez* glinting in the middle of his square beard, coat-tail like a dark anchor holding him down, ideas flying out to all corners of the amphitheatre, some too fast to follow, arcs of equations I copied, baroque proof on the page that the sun can be levered from the earth with a column of tiny numbers.

ÉTUDES GÉNÉRALES, THE SORBONNE

    Simple & colossal enough, Nature's motto: there is no form without destruction of form. But what makes things cluster, & scatter? I was trying to measure the point of minimum awareness of one thing by another. Think of it this way: the cloud of its water. But water that hasn't happened yet. (The great revelations always seemed to exist in the future.) The relentless clustering, the relentless scattering of constellations in the elements – everyday things composed of little lords? – simple & colossal lexicon of embodiment & disembodiment.

"The Curie temperature," Winter 1895

The first time I heard Pierre speak was at the presentation of his thesis, a voice at once grave & youthful, slow & deliberate, an attitude detached yet impassioned toward his subject: the effects of exposing diverse materials to magnetic fields of differing intensities & to thermal excitation. The clarity of his explication seemed to me – & others – the exaltation of human thought. I wanted to know this man. I had seen him once before, a soirée held by Professor Lippmann. He was standing in front of a "French window" giving onto the balcony. He looked much younger than his thirty-five years, due to the absolutely open expression of his face. He was already well known for his work on crystals, & his inventions of several instruments of measurement. One of these had drawn the praise of Lord Kelvin in his experiments on heat & work. We found ourselves face to face one evening in the rue de Chateaudun, on our way back to our respective laboratories. He walked me to the door, asking about my studies, & speaking only briefly of his. I was completing work toward the *license ès mathématiques,* having finished the *license ès sciences* the previous year. I complained of having too little space for my work on magneticism in the Lippmann laboratory. He invited me to use space going begging in the *École municipale de physique et chimie industrielle.* I looked down, away from his bearded face. I couldn't answer. The next day I received a letter from him, with the same invitation. I accepted by return post. Soon we were working together on "thermal excitation." I wanted to say how appropriate the subject was in relation to the feeling for him that was rising in me. (He would later admit to the same thought.) I felt as though I had a continual fever. He suggested sharing an apartment on rue Mouffetard, overlooking a small garden, divided into independent parts. The following spring we were married, at his family home in Sceaux, violets tumbling around us everywhere, tame in the garden & wild in the fields.

Observations, III: Wilhelm Roentgen, Spring 1895

Roentgen believed that description was also an element. He traced what he thought were cathode rays as they streamed from a vacuum tube – the stream sometimes blue, sometimes invisible – to a plate of positive charge. When these rays grazed the glass walls of the chamber, the walls would harbour a green or blue luminescence. Then he packed this vacuum tube in a black cardboard case, but rays could still somehow illuminate a phosphorescent screen *outside* the encased tube. These rays had penetrating power? He placed a number of objects between the tube & a photographic plate, & on each plate, seconds later, there were shadowy "pictures" of the interior of each object. These rays were clever little photographers? He took his wife's left hand. He placed it between tube & plate. Projected there were her delicate, ghostly bones, a smudged ingot marking the marriage ring on her third finger. These weren't cathode rays – they could not be refracted. They were something not yet understood. He called them Xrays.

"The barometer of love," 1896

    A year later, even *Illustration*, usually devoted to saluting the bastions of the Empire, or salivating over royal visits, committed its pages to Xrays: the lacy skeleton of a carp, the coral bones of a frog, a squirrel's walnut-shell skull – these found themselves beside the skeletal hand of Roentgen's wife in a *supplément spéciale*. An Xray pavilion-on-wheels led the Paris Carnival Parade. (Later, there would be "Curie Hair Tonic," for falling hair, "Crema Activa" promising eternal youth, with a bogus note from me that "promised miracles.") At Les Tuileries, a man unveiled a scandalous Xray machine that, for 10 centimes, would measure the strength of our desire.

Henri Becquerel, 1896

> *"One wraps a photographic plate ... in two sheets of very thick black paper ... so that the plate does not fog during the day's exposure to sunlight. A plate of phosphorescent substance is laid above the paper on the outside and the whole is exposed to the sun for several hours. When the photographic plate is subsequently developed, one observes the silhouette of the phosphorescent substance, appearing in black on the negative. If a coin, or a sheet of metal ... is placed between the phosphorescent material and the paper, then the image of these objects can be seen to appear on the negative."*

Becquerel thought it was sunlight causing Uranium salts to phosphoresce, to penetrate that photographic plate. So he took a thin copper cross, slid it between some black paper taped to the photographic plate & the Uranium salts. He expected sunlight to 'photograph' a pattern of the cross on the plate. The sun disappeared for two days, being the sun, in February, in Paris. In the gray light of the third morning, Becquerel developed the plate, expecting to find nothing: no sunlight, no image. But he saw a hazy image of the cross, stark white against the black plate. He lined up everything in a dark cupboard. He came back the next morning. Again, the cross-image was there. Why was no sunlight – no light at all! – needed to produce these photo-graphic impressions? He thought it was the phorescence producing the images. He died, not realizing he had discovered Radioactivity.

And then, nothing. Everyone forgot about Uranium. Everyone was producing Xrays. No one was testing other elements for their power of electrification. Except Kelvin. He showed that Uranium electrified the air. But no one had quantified the energy emitted by Uranium.

I wanted to discover the air's "saturation point." We took two old, wooden vegetable crates, put two metal plates, 8 cm in diameter each, inside, one 3 cm above the other. We placed Uranium salts on the lower plate, & charged it with high voltage.

There's a photo of me from this period, sitting on the cane chair at the wobbly table pulled away from where the rain came through, cylinders, wires, coils spread out over the table. In my left hand a stop watch, in my right the weight I release to produce the charge from Pierre's *quartz piezoélectrique*, the machine Kelvin had called "beautiful."

The Uranium was conducting the charge through the air, from the lower plate to the upper. The speed with which this occurred was determined by the energy emitted by the Uranium. The "saturation point" was reached when no more energy could be released into the air. I surveyed thirteen other elements, but only Pitchblende & Thorium produced currents, currents much stronger than Uranium. They produced rays which travelled, & penetrated. But this defied all the rules of science.

I concentrated on measuring Pitcheblende, the most powerful of the three ray-producing elements. I was sure there was something in it which accounted for its superior emissions. I decided to isolate this substance, whatever it was, by means of extreme heat. We received a shipment of 20 kg of Pitcheblende from the Joachimsthal Mine in October.

I must have looked like a sorceress, stirring a huge pot over a fire all winter in the courtyard, adding more Pitcheblende, stirring, trying to ignore the rain & the cold. At times I would lose all sense of feeling in my hands on the iron bar.

Our paper was read to the Academy in December: "On a new strongly radio-active substance contained in Pitcheblende." Pierre named it Radium. It, too, defied science. In its spontaneity, it produced energy without suffering any change, neither a loss nor a gain of energy. It glowed, & could colour glass, & could penetrate matter.

Once upon a time there was a world of gravity, & then a world of magneticism, & then a world of radioactivity; worlds of rampant exotica, each one stealing logic from the last, & meaning from the next.

Hotel of the Gray Rocks, Port-Blanc, Summer 1897

That village was like a mute factory producing: wind – wind that by day swung down from vast plateaux & cut across the sand, agate & silvered, defacing orange rock-cliffs as it rose from waves transparent & nearly too far below to be heard; wind by night that squirreled low among the cluster of stone houses & the chapel where the skull of St. Gildas cowered in a strongbox like a dull jewel. I was eight months pregnant, but we would often pedal to Brest. Large & awkward, no longer Pierre's *enfanticule*, but carrying one. Once, we had set out in the heat, & had rested in a green gorge with a stream banked with buttercups. Just outside Brest, four young horses pulling carts were so frightened of our bicycles that we were forced to tramp across a ploughed field. The ruts were deep, the muck thick, weighing down our shoes & clogging our wheels. I felt the child churn as we reached the moor above the town, & I was sure she was going to announce herself there, in the light of a huge, yellow moon that had risen suddenly. I pulled up my undershirt, & I shone like a magic cone. We both put our hands there, soft, & felt a supple, almost insubstantial turning. We heard something fall, a brusque thud somewhere in the orchard darkness. Pierre joked it must be the ghost of Newton. It was one of our last moments alone, as only two, our shadows in the moonlight taking on the quality of darkness as if being carried gently inside a mouth.

Irène, 12 September 1897

    I asked for a mirror to be held between my legs, & they thought I was crude. I wanted to see how the body perfectly mantles the body. I wanted to watch the soaked red head poke through, the two precise shoulders shed their elastic satchel, the long, blood-smeared back slide out & legs curl up to the crucial, raw, terrifying spot where we're joined, & cut apart. The clear water of the vase awaiting the cut flower. Myself coming out of my mother. After twelve difficult hours, I wanted to watch the whole moment – we comprehend, don't we, by observing? – the moment when the prize is won & lost to the world; when being is called out, completed in the middle of the call, the natural covering of containment ruthlessly given over to superintendent.

    I detested being protected from Significance. I wanted to see what I could only love open its throat & shape the first note of its argument & splendour. I wanted to see before anyone else what I was responsible for.

INTERNATIONAL CONGRESS OF PHYSICS, PARIS, 1900

    Beside the hard feet of the Eiffel Tower great dynamos in the Palace of Electricity hummed & spun like planets. The hero of the Exposition was inanimate, "magic electric fluid." In a small crowd in a small building beside the American Pavilion, with stern Lord Kelvin in his black suit & hat, Pierre & I watched Loie Fuller dance her famous, gauzy, sinewy dance through jets of electric light tinted gold & green, turned quickly silver & blue & green & blue again by revolving cellophane filters. Her limbs built gorgeous monuments wrecked with dangerous beauty. When the colours changed more & more excitedly, the woman writhed. Lord Kelvin at 73 became his own demonstration of a temperature measured: from under that tight, black bowler a gleaming, circular bead of perspiration came sliding down his temple. A tiny pantomime of Absolute Zero.

Radium, atomic weight 225, 1903

We gathered at Sceaux to celebrate my isolation of one decigram of pure radium chloride, of my fresh determination of its atomic weight. It was a warm evening. We walked out to the garden to admire pleated white-and-pink blossoms on Althea trees. We were distracted by a half-moon looking like a vulnerable sail, or the half-developed photograph of a sail, searching for any boat in a gray, solemn sky. By coincidence, Rutherford had arrived in Paris the day before, from Montréal, & we all joked that he had managed to find us only because he had taken on the properties of his research at McGill: *deflections of like objects by radiation in magnetic fields*. We talked, & laughed, & drank thé à la menthe as the light faded but provided progressively finer definitions of the blossoms on the nearest branch, as if they had become finally what they had to be – fragile, pinkish-white things with a modest aroma, reminiscent of almond, offering no momentary reassurance of their purpose other than that they were flimsy things which lasted only a few days. We sat there hushed, a little taciturn, very little light left, & Pierre, reaching into his waistcoat pocket, said something about how it was supposed to be a celebration &, mimicking a magician, opened a closed fist, in his fist a little tube, which of course I recognized, partly coated with zinc sulphide. He held it out, & suddenly the tube was luminous, a faint lavender glow in the darkness that Rutherford took for Paulonia petals. In the light from the tube, Rutherford could see – we all could see – Pierre's fingers, scarred & inflamed, & that he was finding it hard to keep hold of the tube. I took it out of his hands, carefully, & placed it on the white table as if it were an injured bird. We sat & gazed at it. A fraction of Radium salts in solution. Glowing lavender, darkness descending. Althea blossoms. Pierre's weeping fingers. Rutherford wiping his eyes. A moon no longer having any purpose.

After the Prize

We were the "happy laureates" to the world, but to its reporters we were freaks, brains that reproduced. I was rude. I told them, "You want to write an article on us? But we're not worth an article. We have only existed since yesterday!" So they reproduced a conversation between Irène & the maid. They devoted paragraphs to the black-&-white colours of the cat. Some days, Pierre would give them 15 minutes each, placing his watch mid-point between himself & reporter. He answered merely Yes, he answered merely No. Mounds of letters arrived, every day, for months. Requests for autographs, or money, maudlin praise & prayers, jolly sonnets on Radium, & death-threats, since we had, in discovering Radium, "blasphemed God & unleashed the Devil." An American asked permission to baptize a race horse with my name! It was – an invasion by mindlessness. And when the Academy swung open its massive gates to Pierre & the state offered him the Legion of Honour, those same reporters approached me, his "admirable collaborator," as if I were a dog that could talk: "'Oh, me ! I am only a woman,' she told us smiling. 'No woman, ever, has sat under the Cupola. My only ambition is to aid my husband in his work.'" Which, of course, was utter tripe, utter invention. What I really said was: tell the Minister what we need is not another decoration, but a laboratory. Which, of course, never reached print because they were afraid of offending the office-holders in their turrets & royal corridors, mouthing decrees from their impermanent eternity, ignorant even of the law which allowed them to breathe the air, let alone the law that marks the difference between integration & disintegration, the measure of radiance, to which we all are beholden, unsubject to change.

Meudon, May 1903

We stepped down from the carriage into the idle shadow of the chateau, a shadow darkening only when it reached for the chateau wall & its thick, green-gray leaves, vines of ivy pruned back but still belittling twin windows & the indentation of a door – & there he stood, anchored to the darkest corner of the shadow as it cut across the white-gravel footpath – solemn, stolid, silent as one of his own statues: Rodin. (He had written, in his own hand, sentences plodding across the page like exhausted soldiers, asking if we would consent to visit & explain how "these new rays, as I understand, can penetrate things.") And like one of his statues he bore only one expression, & his was perturbation. Tolerated trespassers. We were, that is, until he took our hands with his own – the fingers I remember as blunt, thick, forceful, like bolts – & led us almost indifferently into his atelier. We saw bodies. Huge, fallen, broken, stripped of all humanity, even unto the sunken eyes. He said one word, *esclaves*, & we felt it like the slap of a parent's hand, & inclined our gaze against our shame, & followed muscled marble straining under the weight of some invisible tyranny into deep folds of stone. Rodin had freed them from some scarce mountain quarry merely to carve them back into this writhing spell of pain? Pain so deep & pure & formal – it was magnificent! Pierre squeezed my arm, & looked terrified. Rodin, haunted. I could feel the stillness around the rippling figures.

Time funnelled me back to a cousin's farm near Lublin, six or seven years old, where I saw four men who had been flayed & horse-dragged dead, left as stiff examples on the farm road to anyone who, like them, might foolishly have wanted a different world.

Rodin let go our hands & took one step toward his slaves. He stared, bewildered, at all that power withering in their limbs & said, "Can they penetrate even this?" as if we thoughtlessly, mistakenly, had discovered a force that could violate art. Pierre looked at me as if to say, *it's useless. He cannot comprehend* …

& then, in defiance of his own doubt, told Rodin
there are, at least, three worlds: one we see & one we do not,
& another, created as they collide, relentless, slave to them both.
    "You must come back," he said.

Royal Institute, London, June 1903

A week earlier, at the Royal Institute in London, I listened as Pierre gave his lecture in the crowded auditorium. (Women could be guests, not lecturers.) He called for the lights to be half-drawn down & showed how Radium affected some photographic plates wrapped in paper. Everyone watched the substance give off visible heat, as Pierre described the medical experiments he had conducted on himself. He had wrapped a specimen of Radium salts in a porous rubber bandage, applied it to his arm, & left it there for 10 hours. We studied the wound. Day by day the salts burned more intensely the skin of his arm. After 52 days, with the removal of the bandage, his arm had acquired a permanent purple-gray scar. "You can still see it," he said. "I like to call it my little cloud." He recalled how Irène was transfixed by this little "cloud" on his arm; how she would study it & want to touch it, & ask all sorts of questions he could not answer. Pierre was fond of ending his lectures by saying that Radium had a million times stronger radioactivity than Uranium. Calling for full lights, he would hold up his bare arm. He would point to the tiny cloud-scar there & say, "Ladies & Gentlemen, tonight you see here on my arm perhaps the beginnings of a cure for cancer."

SCEAUX, JUNE 1905

Irène was with Pierre's father. Forget that it's raining Pierre said to me, taking & unfolding the mauve blanket from the muslin bag strung from the handlebars. And then he spread it out on the rough turf of the pasture beside the path. There were enough clouds that the blonde light could chase itself up the hill & over it, & lift each of the gray stones of the wall that followed the arc of the hill. And what I loved, & what I love to remember, is the nonchalance of his arms, & our speechlessness, & our abandonment of restraint as we hurried to keep warm, beautiful in the rain in that wide, bare pasture.

"Magnetic Properties of Bodies at Diverse Temperatures," July 1903

An object possesses a plane of symmetry, or a plane of reflection. If this plane divides the object into two parts ....

At Millon-la-Chapelle the late violets were autobiographical: *a flower of four petals has a plane of symmetry and an axis of symmetry of the order of two.*

The ponds were almost dry, no lilies, but broom was flowering thick next to the millstone where I removed my underskirt so that Pierre could sit & marshy earth wouldn't leech into his creaky bones. Irène brought us fistfuls of marigolds & by the road through the woods we found ravishing white periwinkles, one among all the rest so perfect we both saw it & immediately plucked it from the bunch for praise & analysis. Pierre twined it into a garland for Irène's blonde hair & charged it with a spell: *piezein piezein.*

Even the finest instrument could not have detected any axis between the two of them, crushing each other with love, the blind pull in one set of cells against the blind pull in the other, one material world to the order of two.

Miscarriage: Convalescence, St. Trojan des Bains, Île d'Oléron, August 1903

Be a scientist, I told myself, one month later: *it was simply a disagreeable beginning which did not become;* causa sui, *the future turning on itself, instants-without-duration, future-without-arrival, therefore: that which could never have been named.* But abstraction could not help. Nor St. Trojan, looking away, out to sea, both hands lost to vandals. It was as though I had lost a prize, a title, *très honorable.* As though I had to try & find myself in the miserly bits of a broken mirror, in the billions of pieces of shells broken at my feet, almost invisible through the disowned froth of the waves.

Solar eclipse, Mont-St-Michel, Summer 1905

    I remember the mad birds circling the Abbey, darkening it & the island, & then, suddenly, stopping, dropping out of sight as the moon became a black monocle for the sun. On the shore we watched through thick lenses Pierre had fashioned from cobalt: the birds' swirling panic over the Abbey's spire, the surface of the sun going iodine. And I remembered my mother reciting Job, daily gasping verses as her lungs filled, & re-filled: *The light is short because of darkness* – one of those wretched Biblical banalities pressed into memory like an ordinary leaf pressed into an ordinary book.

ÈVE, 6 DECEMBER 1905

The unique spiral among the plentiful whirls of thick, black, matted, blood-clotted hair, a spike of formal spontaneity sprouting out of an apple-pattern birthmark just above the pulsing fontanelle marked her, & determined her name: the name of embarkation upon the first fruitful usurping of partnership for experiment's sake; for knowledge's restive procedure, storm & torment, its incorrigible decision *to taste though it be of death* – she looked up at us, & beyond us, with animal eyes from the middle of her dislocated jungle paradise, clearly unconvinced it was a miracle to be here, making chubby fists to prove there were good reasons for her existence that disproved all those that had come before.

St. Remy, Spring 1906

Irène's trick was to scrub her face rosy in Pierre's beard until it burned, then plunge into a cold, salt wave, her face streaked scarlet & white, a petunia surfacing. She'd shake out her wet, sun-whitened hair, & open her blue eyes wide, & her red mouth wide, & shriek, *Papa, je suis ton feu d'artifice!* She'd turn a cartwheel against the double-blue sea-&-sky, & shriek again. Her baby sister frowned. What was the world but a burning face – Irène – burning with what we once were, but had no idea we were: light, particles dispossessed by the perfect laws that made them.

Three Séances: Madame Eusapia Palladino

"These phenomena really exist."
– Pierre Curie, 14 April 1906

She was "The Great Eusapia," renowned for her interventions in the realm of objects & in the realm of the dead. She had travelled the world communicating with ghosts, & had conquered Paris with her supernatural powers. By this time she must have been around fifty years of age. She was heavy-set, wore black crepe, her mouth permanently cast in a severe frown below piercing, unhappy eyes. I met with her once, Pierre several times thereafter…. Out of her arms & legs fluid "members" seeped, exoplasmes that would slither & then leap into the air & vanish. With eyes *écarquillés* she shunted objects from a distance – a table, a chair – & made a ticking clock stop when she blinked, & start when she blinked again. Out of a hole in the side of her head she shot a cold breeze across the parlour, walked a bottle across a table-top, danced a glass up & down the walls. Pierre had Georges Gouy bind her hands & feet. He turned the gas-lamps up so that he could detect any sleight-of-hand, hidden levers, or accomplices. Luminous hands pinched & caressed Pierre's face. He was convinced: "she peopled the void with phantoms." She was to be his next experiment.

Half-Life 1906 – 1914

As unstable atoms are transformed, the radioactivity of a substance decreases. The time required for this activity to decrease by half is called half-life. This half-life is characteristic of any radioactive isotope. It may range from a few fractions of a second to several thousand million years...

Polonium 214	0.164 seconds
Oxygen 15	2 minutes
Iodine 131	8 days
Cobalt 60	5.3 years
Carbon 14	5730 years
Plutonium 239	24,110 years
Uranium 238	4.5 thousand million years

Point of convergence, 17 April 1906

Between Le Palais de Justice & the Pont Neuf, cramped under his black umbrella, thinking, thinking, he walked into gusts along the tree-shadowed quais of the Seine, having passed Place Saint-Michel, with a tender glance at the fountain's lions that Irène & Ève adored, water spewing from their mouths. He ignored the *bouquinistes* closing their stalls, the must of used books absorbing more of the fresh night's coal-smoke. Trams, cabriolets, wagons crammed the Quai Conti. A wagon as long as a chimney, overloaded with bundles of blue military uniforms (braiding on the epaulettes glinting like deadly, gold insects), gained speed, descending mid-way on the bridge. The driver, a milkman named Louis Manin, was making a few extra francs in the evenings driving the wagon, pulled by two huge Percherons. Manin saw a tram coming out of the darkness of the quai, his hands tugged the reins, Pierre stepped over a pot-hole or a puddle, thinking, looking down, Eiffel's tribute to Science lurking above him in the grim distance. The flank of the closest horse brushed him, but the other, rearing, a chess piece poised above the river, sent the wagon skidding, its front wheels missing Pierre entirely, the left rear wheel bringing 1000 kilos to rest on his head, his brains clotted on the collar of his coat, the umbrella twisted useless at his feet.

Pierre, I

They brought me all the things you carried: black fountain pen (the boyish loops of your signature stranded inside it), keys, pocket-book, introduction cards, the watch that didn't stop (cushioned in your waistcoat). They brought me your crumpled umbrella & you, mutilated, separately. Two hours later, in a putrid cart, unrecognizable & almost warm. Still supple, your hand when I kissed it.

AFTER THE FUNERAL, SCEAUX

    I put on my veil again, in order to see everything through my crepe. Into a big fire I threw the tatters of clothes that had been cut away from you, blood flecked with pieces of brain.

Pierre, II: First lecture, the Sorbonne, 5 november 1906

That day, Pierre, I replaced you. What a travesty, even to think it! I knew it was going to be a spectacle I had to deflate: "First Woman Professeur at the Sorbonne." There would be little room for Science in the headlines, & none in that stuffy, terraced lecture hall: just photographers, reporters, "celebrities" – even Countess Greffuhle, overheated in the first row, fanning her neck wrapped in pink silk. It was for my Sèvres students I had to remain impassive, catching my reflection in your glass apparatus: I saw a woman who'd aged 10 years in 6 months – pale face & paler, filmy hair, more ashen now than blonde, pulled back so tight it looked like the coat of some furtive animal; it was to them that I spoke, plainly, because the crowd wanted drama, tears: "When one considers the progress in Physics in the last decade, one is surprised by the changes it has produced in our ideas about electricity & about matter…." But I wanted to tell them I no longer had any ideas about matter: they were buried under the ground at Sceaux; they were splashed on the stones of the Quai Conti; that matter wasn't anything they should believe in, only see through.

Pierre, III

    Before they closed the coffin so they could slide it into the ground, I had to give you one last, horrible kiss on the head, the head you used to offer me, eyes always closed (as they are now, because the moment won't dissipate. Therefore, the hair on your temple & the hair on your beard is still graying). And though the wound was wrapped, on the right side bone jutted out, vivid, still wet & blood-caked. I covered the gauze with flowers & the little photo of me; "petite etudiante bien sage," I could hear you whisper. They packed you in the ditch. Flowers bundled in strewn piles. I put my hand against the coffin & a cold calm – some accumulation of molecules condensing inside? – rushed out & washed over me. Disparate end of everything.

Observations, IV

 I re-read our cahiers. My fingers lolled in the deep depression of your hypotheses printed out so purposefully – as if only a few seconds ago! – in block capitals, like a slow, determined child's. And the observations – phrases impatiently run together, and without signposts: no capitals, no periods, your O's looked like A's, you're A's E's, so that at first my poor eyes had difficulty deciphering some words. (And then I remembered your excitement, writing feverishly in the dark the night we'd returned to rue Lhomand & found the small mounds of our samples, unsheltered in their glass jars on the plain tables & rough boards of our shabby hangar, glowing! That faint but luminous violet light, suspended in clusters, glowing your eery silhouette seated on the cane chair, as you made your rushed entries.) By the end, it was impossible to make out your hand, the words themselves, like shrivelled petals, or pallid patches of scratchy grass in abandoned orchards, the record of crippling phosphoresence. And I remembered your skin, peeling, & for years, re-peeling. And how, when I kissed them, unfolded them from their grip on the emptiness in your coffin, I saw how even in death the frayed ends of your fingers had retained the intense purple of hydrangeas.

In the mountains

    Sleigh horses shook with excitement, took steps at first so short their shoulders shuddered, then easily pulled me along a corridor of rutted snow & wet, black oaks, ghostly lindens, scrags of mistletoe. There was no one to kiss. No one to notice (at exactly the same moment) how a branch can burnish with its shadow the sharp edge of a drift blue. No one to lift the phenomenal above itself: quietly observe how one thing can restore another, make it more "real" through its own loss; ask the question whether or not this is a jubilant donation or accident of oblivion.

Pierre, IV

    I couldn't tell if I was dreaming or if it was early morning or if I'd never slept through the heavy stupor of half-dark, & threatening lightning. A tangible, terrible electricity in the air. Your head materialized: suspended, swollen, empurpled, eyes gone back so that only white showed, your bearded face a bunch of figs mashed on the street after the market's gone, & then a face with dignity somehow expressing disgust with itself. But when you saw me looking, hoping … there was only blankness, not even wrinkles of meaning as the light grew, or the dream ended, your mouth half-open, then gaping, dark, & vulgar.

Recovering, Pierre, V

I gave the children over to Bronia & returned to St Rémy, the last place we slept together. I received a card with a small letter from a poet, a Monsieur Valéry, lodging nearby. I couldn't face a soul, not especially a poet, & I'm afraid I was brutally curt in my reply: "I am interested in things, not in persons." It was an echo of the last sentence I spoke to you, not a sentence of love & tenderness but a reproach that kept tightening like a tourniquet around my throat. The village light was thawing into spring, but not even warmer winds could kill the chill of diminution: you were a set of dates.

St Malo, evening walk, low tide, summer 1908

    The girls were beautiful with evening catching in the waves of their hair. When they ran ahead of me along the shore they seemed farther away than was possible, half-way to Infinity. Pierre called them Bébé Prime & Bébé Square, animated integers, their cellular algebra something like the atom's – the physics of random coupling determined from the start.

Rejection: La Candidature Féminine, L'Académie Française, 1910

"May women not denature themselves! May they not demand from masculine ambitions the satisfactions which would not fulfill them.... They were created only for love, they can live only by it; let them try not to forget." *Le Figaro*, 4 January 1910

They really did think I was a sorceress – my instruments threatened their ceremonial swords – a witch dabbling in magical caprices. And when I protested, & put my name forward, & reminded them that science is a feminine word, they called me "Our Lady of the Tear in the Eye," unworthy of wearing the green gown, unworthy of joining *les Immortels*. The press claimed the public had balked at my "lack of reserve." Indeed, it was a "lack" – the lack of self-effacement, the lack of sly coquetry, the lack of a perfumed sachet dangling from my waist. They smelled the sweat of work on me, not the powders of Marianne, darling of the Republicans. I would have marked the end of their two hundred & fifteen year-old world, a stray comet smashing through the palace's barred & bolted doors.

PIERRE, VI, BETRAYAL

I decided *I* would be the next experiment. Object: to discover the charge I could receive from another pair of hands, another mouth. I slid my pallid body (will you forgive it?) between the blanket & Paul Langevin's pallid body. Oh, the phosphorescence of his face! It was good that it was dark. (No sunlight, no image.) The small gold cross glinting from his neck circled above me like a coil when he moved. And it stayed there, circling in front of my eyes days after on the clear plate of the air, vortex of anticipation, current of delinquency & betrayal, bright symbol christening the theory that passion will exhaust reason every time.

The Duel, 11:00 a.m., 26 November 1911, Bois de Vincennes

It is the noblest of male rituals, and the noblest way to possess good blood lines is to endanger one's own blood.
  – Emile Bruneau de Laborie, The Laws of the Duel, 1906

When it comes to speaking of duels, we should always remember the joke about the journalist's wife who couldn't find her husband and was worried to death – until she learned he'd travelled to the countryside to fight a duel.

"*Grace à Dieu!*" *she cried*
"*He's safe!*"
  – Le Petit Journal, 1905

I'm sure that Paul wanted that pistol to end it all heroically … but what a cowardly farce! – the two of them arriving, like stupefied birds at the last moment, having both gotten lost in the foggy trails of the Bois, then scurrying to their marks so as not to be labelled late & uncourageous, both bundled up against the cold in *chapeaux melons*, black coats, scarves tight around collars turned up in November's damp. Seconds marked off the field, thirty paces, then handed over loaded chambers. (Off to one side, pigeons were picking at the ground.) The Director informed the "noble adversaries" of the rules & then, from under a waxed mustache his voice bleated, "Gentlemen! You are ready?! One, two, three, fire!" But Gustave Tery pointed his pistol at the ground, & Paul, seeing this, his arm half-lifted, lowered his as well. A long, painful silence. The Seconds conferred. The Director consulted. An agreement was signed by both parties. The Seconds re-conferred. The pistols were fired into the air for the benefit of the photographers. The attending physicians snapped their black bags shut. The duel was over. I was in Sweden, accepting the Prize. But I had to come home & read this account of how I had destroyed a family, how his wife & children had been abandoned, how "France barely missed being deprived of a precious brain." I'd had enough of brains, & the loss of brains. I wanted the vast, empty gray brain of the sea.

THE OFFER

Goodbye – to my naïve surprise when I learned of Paul's return to his wife. And goodbye to my appreciation of irony's panache when I learned of her acquiescence to a mistress because she was "average," a secretary, and French. Goodbye sorrow, goodbye revenge. Goodbye second love, second loss of second love. Goodbye forgiveness & the offer of its unimaginably tiny pleasure.

Les Voitures Radiologiques: The Great War 1914-1918

BRETAGNE, 1 AUGUST 1914

At L'Arcouëst all summer every morning: bronze rocks, raw-green sea, empty-clothesline horizon. A sky so calm the girls & I could have swum it to the island, but took instead its reflection, sailed quickly across on the Eglantine, singing French & Canadian songs. Every morning, that is, until the morning when we learned that Jaurès, good Jean Jaurès (now our Panthéon companion) had been murdered in Paris the night before, & so we could not move – all kindness, all sympathy, all warmth seemed to have been killed. The weather turned cold. And if that news wasn't enough to deaden the day, to give the date a heartless infamy & slur us into monotone, the evening's announcement at *la mairie* chilled us into silence. *This afternoon, at 3:45, the Republic of France mobilized its armed forces.*

Soon there would be Verdun, Amiens, Eparnay, Montdidier, mustard gas, the Somme, the Marne, rivers of mud & blood.

SUMMER HEAT, PIERRE, VI

The cruel admixture of sleeplessness & dream, those horses' heads breathing down stable-stench hot into my face, so I bashed their heads into the stones of the wet street, desperate nostrils steaming, eyes glaring terrified boiled medallions. Me suddenly with a calm, dutiful face. Me with a black club in my hands, turning away from them, turning, expecting to find my obstinate husband standing in the gusty rain, thinking. An accident that has no hope of happening.

FROM THE LIGHTHOUSE

 I remember looking up from a letter I was writing & seeing the long column of light swing across the sea like a sword. In the dark trees, it looked like an eye, opening & closing, or the breast of a bird taking flight, in a palpitation of fear. With each sweep of sword-light my breath would catch. Troops were massing on both sides of the German border. The Kaiser had announced that his troops would return, victorious, "before the leaves have fallen from the trees."

La Voiture Radiologique

After only two weeks: the dead uncountable, the wounded stacked in fly-covered sheds – amputated, blind, insane. Soon I was driving the *voiture radiologique* into the artillery's aftermath, that dark-red throat of mud & moans & blood-soaked canvas stretchers. Irène patched black cables to a generator, covered the windows with black curtains. I unfolded the table, installed the silver ampoule, called for the wounded:

Tardy, Emile. Fourteenth Chasseurs.   Photographed. Xray no. 1384 Bullet in forearm (left). Removed   depth 1/2 cm. Decouzon, Jean-Baptiste. 263rd Infantry. Pain left leg (thigh, upper) Photographed (great difficulty, much shrieking) Xray no. 1385 Shell fragment removed   depth 10 cm.

And drive again, the weight of the hours & of the apron's lead having deadened my shoulders (though sometimes I'd photograph without it, the men being in such pain, there were so many, & no time …) 130 km along the Somme I collapsed, men trudging past, sopping packs dripping rain into mud, crude crosses made from blanket scraps & branches floating with rats bloated in the zig-zag trench. Uncountable? Uncountable like leaves. 60,000 Englishmen falling in one day.

Unknown (unidentifiable, still breathing, unconscious) Photographed. Xray no. 6266 shell fragment under scapula penetrated external face of arm & axilla. shell fragment. left lung. shell fragment. right shoulder. bullet. fibula (right). bullet. face (right & left sides),

Driving at dawn, always the scar of the trench, men walking calmly toward it like penpushers to the office, a sharp turn toward Argonne, a fairy forest, riderless horses among the silence of atoms harmless in flowers, grass, trees.

Near the Line

    I got rapidly used to it. Gunfire & shelling a few hundred meters from German lines. (In the calm, you could hear them laughing, or coughing.) The men lived in vicious families, keeping house in the trench, fighting each other's claims on useless things scavenged from farms abandoned months earlier: a broken table, a three-legged chair, ratty card-deck, oil-lamp, oily mattress. Masked sentries walked the cross-hatched branches of the floor, though hard rain sent all this swirling away, ragged flags & dead bodies.

L'HÔTEL DE LA NOBLE ROSE: FURNES, BELGIUM, DECEMBER 1914

The rooms were mostly rubble, & there were no roses. The Germans had levelled everything, & the one thousand English soldiers who had come to save "la brave petite Belgique" were dead, except for one hundred thirty-seven, mangled & marked with black-ink crosses on their skin, radioscoped so the surgeons could know where to go in. King Albert drove an ambulance jammed with men to the hospital at Hoogstade. I was pleased Irène could meet a king with a heart. When we arrived there, only one soldier had come through surgery, which had taken seven hours – small projectiles in the face, throat, one arm gone – & somehow he asked to see me, to offer his thanks for our help. He introduced himself, politely, as if the small, painful gurgling in his throat did not exist. His name was Reginald Smith, twenty-one years, a Canadian from the west of that country, a place called Winnipeg, & he had enlisted, thinking the war would last only a year, as a way of seeing his fiancée in London. (He had left her behind, & hoped to bring her to Canada after establishing himself there.) He gave me two packets of letters – one for his family in Winnipeg, one for his fiancée in London. He asked would I write a note to both – now that he no longer had his writing hand! – saying that he would certainly be seeing them as soon as the healing of his wounds would permit. He said his little brother Maurice would be pleased & proud to receive a word from a Nobel-prize winner. Of course, I agreed, & sent my letters with his to the family & the fiancée. I said that Reginald Smith had died a valiant death. And I wrote them that he felt no pain; that a single bullet had stopped his heart, & that he was at his death a handsome young man in his uniform who would certainly be receiving the highest honour from their king for his sacrifice. He was a wounded thing. Ligament strings gaped out from the pulp where his shoulder oozed to a rank stump. He had stopped talking, my hand asleep on the blood-caked bar of his stretcher, & he had become abruptly old. Something greedy had begun to eat whatever still passed for life in him. I felt a sick arousal in the air. There was the smell of cordite & ointment, the silence of that impatient feeding – of the present on the past – on a pale, useless body.

Driving: Creil to Montereau, Montereau to Mormont, October 1917

I was at times the only thing living, driving among the avenues of the dead: the trenches, those perfect receptacles for nationalistic surge & spillage; long boulevards of bodies, neatly laid out, reaching farther than history could hope to reach through the treeless mud. All that anonymity, all that blankness in their upturned eyes – the blankness of countries under a vast, borderless snow. I saw myself as some old crone, poking with a stick at bloated abdomens, searching for valuables, scanning the hands for rings, the necks for crucifixes in gold. It was a dream so real I could hear the gas escaping from their mouths, that alien alchemy, bromides & sulphides they'd breathed into themselves the instant before they stopped being themselves. I woke up with fists gripping the wheel like white fossils. The small glittering of dew on the windscreen was an emblem: a cluster of crystal islands marking the sad transparency of knowledge, & the extinction of knowledge, of the thinking, terrifying brain divided infinitesimally into its lonely parts; the rampant swirl of perishing atoms which are nothing but solace temporarily organized against its inevitable, logical breakdown, half by half by half, until all knowledge becomes a myth of the Living for the Dead & we become their accidental discovery – of a tense not the present, the future, or the past.

Sister Prometheus 1918 – 1937

The decay of the atom is the decay of the world. The thickest walls have suddenly collapsed. Everything has become uncertain, unsteady, fluid. I would not have been surprised if a stone had been pulverized in the air in front of me and had suddenly become invisible.

– *Wassily Kandinsky, Journals*

Diviner

"Science, severe and inexorable science…"
— Charles Richet

One gram of radium heats one gram of water from freezing to boiling in under one hour. Knowing this, everything, everything, changed. The rare world shivered as we stole its invisible overcoat. Even if we'd wanted to, we could never have given it back.

The Solvay Conference, Brussels, 1911

Einstein, Planck & I met over tea on the hotel terrace to discuss Nernst's quantum contradictions. Planck, I learned, was blunt, intractable, dispassionate, slurping his tea, asserting that "'Life' is, was, & always will be a quite literal *matter* of rampant disintegration." Einstein laughed politely at this *mauvais jeu de mots*, but said later that there was another way of looking at it. We were quite alone, walking along the edge of a lake, Einstein in his dented Homburg, his great fur coat with pins for buttons, his lips musing at the end of his pipe-stem. Both eyebrows scuttled over drooping lids like trapped crayfish. "Perhaps Planck is wrong." "'Life'" could be, he said, "the continual revision of a gorgeous elegy."

OBSERVATIONS, VI: HIKING, SWITZERLAND, MAY 1912

    We had agreed to hike Engadine, an Alpine pass, which Einstein seemed to think would be equal to a stroll through Lausanne. He ambled along like a pregnant cat, squinting, nursing theories with his son, Hans, & flirting with Anna, our English governess, distracting her from the children at every glacier mill along the path, explaining to her "Nature's hidden forces," & not very successfully concealing his own. He recited names of surrounding peaks, looking at her as if she were a fresh egg & he'd not eaten in a week. I slipped into a watchful silence not even Irène's cold stare could pull me out of. Our stopping, & starting, & stopping was some crude drama of discontinuity, of the meadows of molecules Einstein was always strolling through, always pausing among, casting in the glassy lakes for a secret he wasn't fully aware he was trying to catch, & weigh, & measure, & throw back, preferring the measurements for example, of Anna's hips, of his own longing to be delivered from the reality of the instant & nothing but the instant; preferring to imagine the secret curriculum under her smock rather than anything which would eventually bear his name in classrooms & laboratories, betrothed only to her neck & shoulders, to what he could see of her flesh, the arsenal of Swiss light bending moment-by-moment down over peaks beside blue lakes to rest the eons of its granulated, epic arc finally, & momentarily magnanimous on her face & throat, her throat's pulse – what the whole circumstance of light & desire had led to: Einstein's aroused brain extending its aging fingertips....

OBSERVATIONS, VII: LECTURE, BERLIN, FEBRUARY 1923

I stepped down on to the platform & regretted my decision immediately: a crowd was rolling toward me, flashbulbs *poc poc*, notebooks flapping, pencils poised like small weapons.

But they rushed right past me, almost knocking me down. They were there to welcome the boxer, Dempsey, who had been on the same train. He was there to fight the German champion. But frankly, he looked more frightened than I had been, tame as a Daschund, his white fists folded meekly in front of him, trying to avoid contact of any kind.

Gifts: Trans-Atlantic Tour, United States, 1929

I returned exhausted, but with one gram of Radium. It was worth 100,000 American dollars. Ève was at the station to meet me, no one else — no cameras, no reporters — since I'd arranged to return in secret. We took a hansom cab to the apartment on Île St Louis. The concierge dragged my valises up the three flights, where we unpacked their contents: five pointed copes of dark velvet & bright silk, eleven medals in eleven leather boxes, eight rolls of parchment, doctorates *honoris causa* and the most precious (after the Radium) — a dozen banquet menus, their stiff cardboard backs perfect for making calculations, thick shards of petrified Texas wood, to be used as paperweights, one sharp blade of damascene from Toledo for cutting the pages of unread books, two crude wool carpets by Polish mountaineers living now in Chicago, and around my neck a string of turquoise stones, inlaid with Indian-silver lightning. Irène wanted to hear all about the day with President Harding, the presentation of the Radium in Pittsburgh. But what she enjoyed most was hearing about how, on the trip across, I was discovered by the steward, in the wardrobe of my room, standing stupefied in the dark, trying to understand how the automatic light worked.

In the Bibliothèque Nationale

I always liked to keep a little vial of Radium salts by the bed. It shone in the darkness & I could write legibly if woken in the night by an idea. Even now, if you consult my three black notebooks in the Bibliothèque Nationale, you sign a certificate that you do so at your own risk. People will be signing certificates for at least one thousand six hundred & twenty years, until the evidence of my fingers begins to fade, but only by half from the same pages you can touch with your own.

Cataracts

  Gradually, everything came to be veneered with a dusty rain: the engraved scale of the chronometer, a blackboard filled with equations, the edges of some stairs. My watch-face took on the lustreless sheen of a coin. There was a wisp of frost trespassing on the lens of the microscope. The figures in the workbooks of my students looked like small spills. It was as though I'd grown slowly illiterate. Words were strange if they seemed anything other than overcast skies. But there were advantages to these little glaciers spreading across each iris: I saw only half the wrinkles I used to see in the mirror. And the price of everything was the same. The idea of nothing, of zero, so steadfast, so taciturn, ordering things, was reassurance that emptiness could be enough to produce wonder.

Radium Necrosis, 1925

Look at my fingers, scarred & gnarled. How could I have known? – I was so proud of my Emanation Service, Radium ampoules at the Front: all those soldiers injected for loss of blood, to loosen joints, to stimulate 'nerve function': How could I have known? I do remember reading about Edison's assistant – the cancer – but how could I have known? Then Demalander & Deminitroux, dead within four days of each other, buried with Thorium X coating their lungs. Nine dead American women, luminous watch-dial painters from New Jersey, 'pointing' their brushes with their moist lips – this made of me a dubious martyr, "Our Lady of Radioactivity."

Lapse, 1932

    I stared fixedly at the teacup, at the spoon in the teacup, which became a glass rod, & I asked Irène "was it done with Radium or Mesathorium?" Irène squeezed my hand & there was no teacup, no spoon, no glass rod, no sorrow coating my eyes.

Death, 3 July, 1934

It's hard to remember now. Rain was expected. But that had already clouded my eyes. I had to be helped to bed, a last time. The dumb humming in my ears would not stop. I demanded to read my temperature on the thermometer. I could not read the temperature on the thermometer because my hand was shaking. Ève saw that my temperature had dropped. Because my hand was shaking, I could feel recovery blossom. It's difficult to remember if the rain fell before or after I squinted at the blurred line of mountains. Was it rain that made them come unhinged, one by one? Silver light swelled on the window then thinned out around my face, though I'm not sure, because it was listless, indifferent, & the perimeter of grief in the room cindered the rain, brittle on the roof, leaving nothing even in its calculations.

Train to Sceaux: Burial, 4 July, 1934

Think of dying as being on a train, the engine bearing away one coach, your body on the train seat, staring out the window until the engine switches rails, advances into the future & you stay stopped against the abutment of the present, the myth of mechanical laws. You wait patiently for movement, that first, slow lurch & tug suggesting revolution, wheels wrenching you out of fatality. Shadows ravage the window, then night, piece by piece, falls out of each star's gold scrap-basket. You set off on foot. Your coat is black, too warm to wear, but light to carry.

BONE MUSIC: EXHUMATION, 1995

When they forced open my coffin in their gasmasks & gowns of lead, they looked like tribal priests from another planet. They passed their Geiger wands over the black fabric of a musty dress & veil, the yellowed bones underneath, measuring the music still echoing from the small funerals for each pore, for each cell from cranium to sacrum, the everlasting music of Radium's reprimand, its tongue-clicking reproach. Goodbye to that half of me. Goodbye to the vertebrate ladder ascending to the jaw-bone set like a trap, the phantom voice asking anyone who wants to contend with identity: "Don't you recognize me?" – Master of Female Half-Truths.

Millennium Eclogue, L'An 2000

I could feel light fading in a feebly luminous silhouette. Fading from the parlour of our Nowalipki apartment, & out of the dark mahogany table where Papa would sit & translate Dickens to Mama, recite to us the cadences of Michiewicz & Kransinski; fading out of the French china cup always so near his right hand, the cup painted with bright yellow Bourbon lilies on one side & a rosy torso of Louis Philippe on the other; seeping out of the green marble table inlaid with quartz in gray & yellow, the patterns of a chessboard; fading from the face of the staid old bishop on the wall, a portrait, supposedly, by Titian; sagging out of the silver column of mercury in the barometer Papa hung like a crucifix in his study (which smelled like the pipe-smoke in his hair); out of my very first memory of my very first understanding that I could think, which returned in a dream during the days of measuring fraction after fraction of Radium: I am staring at blocks piled neatly in the toychest of our room, the children's room. I take my greatest pleasure, which is to topple the chest & imagine the wisdom of the blocks as they choose, each one of them, where they should come to rest – each a different colour, each colour a different shape – & come to rest exactly *there*. I could feel the century's energy sliding out of shale on the slopes of the Tatras; oozing up into dank air above the banks of the Vistula, though it clings to muck & garbage, as it does on the banks of the Seine, even in the wake of a slow *peniche* lugging slag under its bridges; out of the bridges of the Seine themselves; out of their blonde stone; their arcs; gargoyles, gaunt or saucy, gazing down at tourists in Bateaux Mouches; out of the beaks of baguettes in the boulangeries along rue de Tour; out of the cobblestones of rue Mouffetard where I slept in the *chambre de bonne* under the Mansard roof, eating turnips or potatoes, a half-square of chocolate for energy when water in the basin froze during the night; where I studied under the covers, fully dressed, the gaslamp failing & the room turning gray, & then the windows.

Squeals of a late wagon-axle would rise up from the street as footsteps on the dark stairs outside the door would falter before I could tell, coming out of sleep, if they were ascending or descending. Out of the spires of churches, & children's shoes, & the hair of magistrates & the pressed suits of politicians; out of theorems scratched on notepads, aloof, sad but clear, almost completely lifeless, like ancient gossips who manage to stay alive because they know, & love deeply the fact that they know, there is nothing happening that they won't eventually discover.

Disappearance: The 500 franc note

Not quite how we pictured ourselves: decapitated by La Banque de France. Authenticated by laser-activated water-marks, authorised by the signatures of Le Secretaire, Le Contrôleur, Le Cassier. Our shrunken heads crumpled into pocketbooks, snapped out of billfolds, abandoned on soiled restaurant table-cloths. We held our colour but not our value. The Euro has succeeded. You can no longer rub our faces thoughtfully between your fingers.

The Craters of Maria

Lat: 18.2° S, Long: 95.5° E   Diameter: 127 km
– *Clementine* Mission (the Moon)

Lat: 2.8° W, Long: 33.8 N   Diameter: 116 km
– *Viking Orbiter* Mission (Mars)

    What is the mind but ongoing agitation? – a small planet with origins of the planet at its core, the earthly & unearthly pleating the brain, its dimpled wrinklings laden even in its dubious hollows with star-spoor & bog-moss; spongy marble, a sacristy unknowingly assembled, hung here, unsolicited, by gravity, out of the strewn molecules of never then & never yet … There are empty seas on the moon, the frozen canals of Mars – rarefied matter in perpetual postponement, gaps in the story, but only two gaps, among the billions. The mind a gap, too, when it shrinks toward the intractable, as it spins slowly away from the subject of its breathing, its turning, out of range of ideas & the hearing of its own voice warn that it's slipping, back toward its meaningless *thereness*, a crater free of purpose…

Le Panthéon, II, Apotheosis

    We wait for the hour when sunlight abandons the dome & its final rays stop pencilling through the small, rectangular windows of the great door, & the clerk begins tidying information brochures in the bevelled rack beside *la caisse*, while another clerk stuffs money in a green canvas sack, Admission Cinq Euros, the soiled sign leans sadly against the glass. After the last clopping echo of the last tourist dies, broom-whisks push litter & street-grit that has blown in & settled under floormats – gray, damp, sodden – back out onto the top step of the twenty more that lead down from fluted columns to rue Clotilde; after it has been silent enough for Geneviève to come for us, lighting the stairs with her lantern up to the Cupola, & the scene of her Apotheosis, & after she leaves to make her rounds, we watch Atila cross the Rhine & turn his men away from Nanterre toward Orléans, & he doesn't know why. He doesn't know there is a young woman named Geneviève on her knees behind the puny walls of Nanterre who has assured the doubtful elders that God will protect them. It happens the same way every evening in Gros's fresco: Faith stalls History's mad swirl, turns it aside like a fragile dam, & thousands in one city rejoice while thousands in another die. The dead are scattered across the bottom of the fresco, verdant hills cradling their neo-classical haunches. The dead look so alive, as if someone knew every one of their names, & called them, name by name. And so we come evenings, after heavy casualties, to help them open their eyes in order to make their way across the river, because it seems to us a little unrealistic of Gros to have left the eyes half-closed like that.

CODA

What I would never have known how to say alive, I know how to say here, on the other side of discovery, informed by the rigour of dying, which is the continuous gathering of the blue-&-cinder-coloured mineral Absence, jubilant we have no bruises or wounds, no pain except for the loss of the world – its masonry of desire & failure – which is not any loss at all, except for the precipitate of the honeycombed brain, preparing & calming the confused heart on its way out: *Now there is only interim, no whole, no half, no measure of beginning decomposing even before it's begun. Now we gather nothing & take no notice. This is what we thought of, in the blurred landscape of the previous age, as* Mercy.

ACKNOWLEDGEMENTS

I am grateful for the help offered me by everyone in the Muzeum Marii Sklodowskiej-Curie in Warsaw, in particular its Director, Ms Malgorzata Sobieszczak-Marciniak; and to the Musée Curie, Paris, especially its director, Mme Soraya Boudia. Much gratitude also to Brian Spence and his Abbey Bookshop, La Librairie Canadienne de Paris, for friendship and inspiration.